ZEBRAS

Published by Creative Education, Inc., 123 South Broad Street, Mankato, Minnesota 56001

Printed by permission of Wildlife Education, Ltd.

Library of Congress Cataloging-in-Publication Data

Wood, Linda C., 1945-
Zebras / by Linda C. Wood.
p.   cm. — (Zoobooks)
Summary: Examines the behavior, habitat, and different kinds of zebras.
ISBN 0-88682-420-6
1. Zebras—Juvenile literature. [1. Zebras.] I. Title. II. Series: Zoo books (Mankato, Minn.)
QL737.U62W66   1991   599.72'5—dc20   91-2821 CIP AC

EBRAS

Series Created by
John Bonnett Wexo

Written by
Linda C. Wood

Zoological Consultant
Charles R. Schroeder, D.V.M.
Director Emeritus
San Diego Zoo &
San Diego Wild Animal Park

Scientific Consultant
Oliver Ryder, Ph.D.
Geneticist, Research Department
Zoological Society of San Diego

Art Credits

All paintings by Richard Orr. **Activities Art** by Nick Corleoné.

Photographic Credits

Front Cover: © Frans Lanting; **Pages Six and Seven:** M. P. Kahl (DRK Photo); **Page Eleven: Top,** Maresa Pryor-Adams (Animals Animals); **Right,** © Frans Lanting; **Page Thirteen:** Zoological Society of London; **Pages Fourteen and Fifteen:** Stephen J. Krasemann (Photo Researchers); **Inside Back Cover:** Gregory G. Dimijian, M.D. (Photo Researchers).

Our Thanks To: Carol Barsi (Natural History Museum); Wendy Perkins (San Diego Zoo Library); Bernard Thornton; Joe Selig.

Contents

Zebras _____ 6-7

Most zebras live on the open grasslands, ____ 8-9

A zebra's life is full of danger _____ 10-11

At first glance, _____ 12-13

Zebras are social animals. _____ 16-17

Zebras are grazing animals _____ 18-19

Baby zebras are called foals_____ 20-21

Zebra's fun _____ 22-23

Index_____ 24

Zebras are among the most beautiful animals on earth. With their bold black and white stripes, they stand apart from every other kind of animal. In Africa, where all zebras live today, thundering herds of these magnificent animals roam freely over the vast plains.

Many people don't know it, but zebras are actually one of the only true wild horses left in the world today. All horses, both domestic and wild, belong to the animal group with the scientific name *Equus* (EE-kwis).

Like all horses, zebras have long, handsome faces with big, gentle eyes. They have strong bodies and long, slender legs. And once they get going, they can run with a speed and grace that is truly wonderful to watch.

But that's where the similarities end. Zebras are shorter than most other horses, and they have smaller hooves. Their manes are stiffer, and their ears are larger. But most important, *only* zebras have stripes—*even their manes are striped*!

As you will see, there are three different types of zebras—and each type lives in a different part of Africa. *Plains zebras* are found in east and central Africa on the open grasslands and along the edges of deserts. *Mountain zebras* live in the stony mountains of southern Africa. And *Grevy's zebras* (GREV-eez) live in the dry semi-deserts of northeast Africa.

Plains zebras are the most common zebras. There are more than 300,000 of these animals in Africa today. But there are far fewer Grevy's zebras, and *even fewer* Mountain zebras. Just 30 years ago, *millions* of these animals crowded the African plains. Why have so many zebras disappeared?

The biggest reason is that people have turned the wild lands into farms and ranches. This limits the amount of open space where zebras can run free. Another reason is unlawful hunting. Many zebras have been killed for their beautiful skins.

Fortunately, things are being done to protect zebras now. African governments and wildlife organizations have set up nature preserves, where zebras can live without the risk of being hunted. This is an important step toward saving these beautiful animals in the wild.

Most zebras live on the open grasslands, where there is plenty to eat—but few places to hide from predators. To stay alive, they must be able to *make a quick getaway* when a predator creeps up.

The legs of zebras are very long, so when they run they can take big strides. And they have strong muscles and large lungs, so they can keep running for long distances without tiring or slowing down.

Zebras are plant-eating animals, or *herbivores* (URB-eh-voars). As you will see below, they have extra long necks to help them reach the grass on the ground. And they have special teeth to help them chew their food.

A zebra has several speeds, or *gaits*. Each gait requires the animal to move its legs in a different pattern. The most important gaits for running are the *trot* and the *gallop*.

When grazing, zebras use their sharp front teeth like scissors to clip off the grass. Usually, they eat only the tips of the grass.

The bones of a zebra are lightweight, but strong. As thin as a zebra's leg may look, it is actually strong enough to support all of the animal's weight when it gallops. And zebras are heavy—some weigh as much as 950 pounds (430 kilograms).

The strong back teeth, or *molars*, are used to crush and grind coarse grass. When chewing, the lower jaw moves against the upper jaw in a sideways motion. A zebra's back teeth keep growing until the animal reaches old age, so they almost never wear out.

MESOHIPPUS
(ZEBRA ANCESTOR)

MODERN ZEBRA FOOT

MESOHIPPUS FOOT

Zebras' early ancestors had three toes on each foot—as did the ancestors of all members of the horse family. Modern zebras have *only one toe* on each foot—surrounded by a hard hoof.

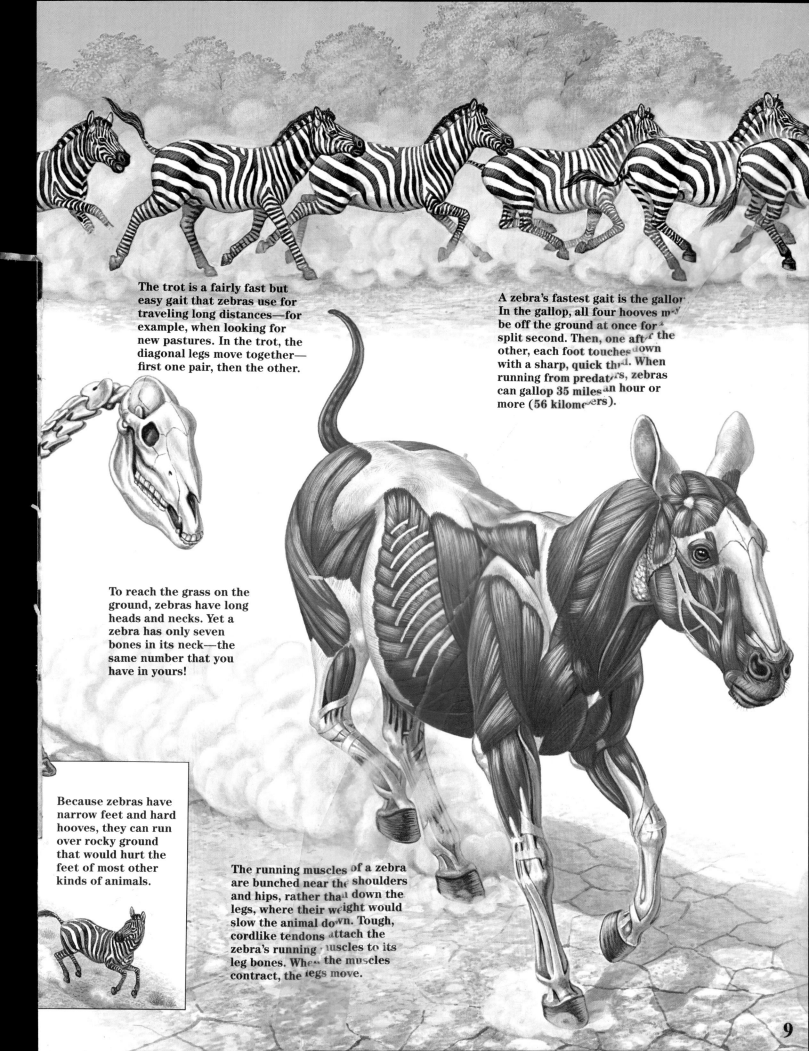

The trot is a fairly fast but easy gait that zebras use for traveling long distances—for example, when looking for new pastures. In the trot, the diagonal legs move together—first one pair, then the other.

A zebra's fastest gait is the gallop. In the gallop, all four hooves may be off the ground at once for a split second. Then, one after the other, each foot touches down with a sharp, quick thud. When running from predators, zebras can gallop 35 miles an hour or more (56 kilometers).

To reach the grass on the ground, zebras have long heads and necks. Yet a zebra has only seven bones in its neck—the same number that you have in yours!

Because zebras have narrow feet and hard hooves, they can run over rocky ground that would hurt the feet of most other kinds of animals.

The running muscles of a zebra are bunched near the shoulders and hips, rather than down the legs, where their weight would slow the animal down. Tough, cordlike tendons attach the zebra's running muscles to its leg bones. When the muscles contract, the legs move.

A zebra's life is full of danger from hungry lions, leopards, hyenas, and wild dogs. Most of the time, these predators hunt by sneaking up on their prey, and then catching it by surprise. To be safe from them, zebras must *stay alert at all times*.

Luckily, zebras have wonderful senses to help them detect enemies *before* they attack. Their excellent eyesight, hearing, and sense of smell all help to warn them when predators are nearby.

When a zebra is attacked, it will fight for its life—kicking hard with its hind legs and biting with its teeth. A zebra can kill a leopard with one well-placed kick. But often it is the leopard that wins the fight.

A zebra can easily outrun a predator over a long distance. As it runs, it zig-zags from side to side, looking back over its shoulder to see if the predator is still behind it. If it can get away in the first 100 yards (90 meters), it is usually home free.

Zebras have excellent hearing to listen for predators. They can twist their flexible ears in almost any direction to pick up sounds all around them.

The eyes of a zebra are set high on the *sides* of its head—to allow a wide range of vision. Even when bending down to graze, zebras can look out over the tops of the grass and watch for predators.

When two zebras stand side by side, they usually face in opposite directions. This makes it possible for them to see in *all directions*—and makes it twice as easy to spot predators.

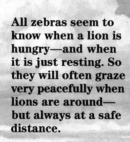

All zebras seem to know when a lion is hungry—and when it is just resting. So they will often graze very peacefully when lions are around—but always at a safe distance.

Danger lurks everywhere for zebras—even in the water. A hungry crocodile in a waterhole will grab a zebra in a second if it has a chance.

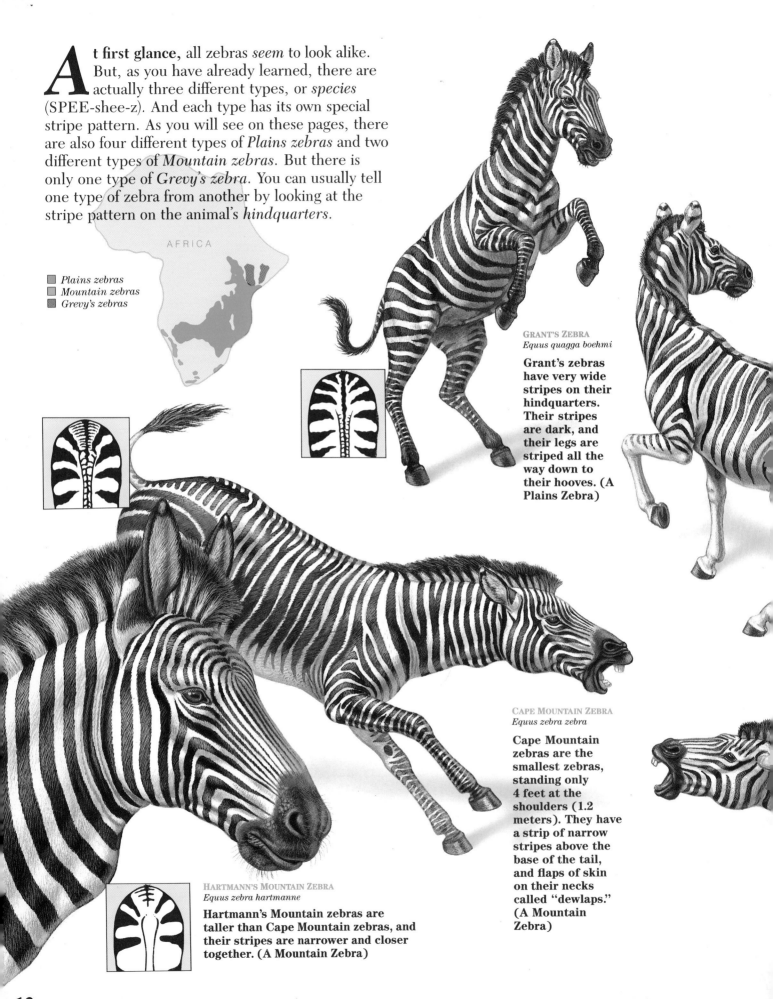

At first glance, all zebras *seem* to look alike. But, as you have already learned, there are actually three different types, or *species* (SPEE-shee-z). And each type has its own special stripe pattern. As you will see on these pages, there are also four different types of *Plains zebras* and two different types of *Mountain zebras*. But there is only one type of *Grevy's zebra*. You can usually tell one type of zebra from another by looking at the stripe pattern on the animal's *hindquarters*.

AFRICA

- Plains zebras
- Mountain zebras
- Grevy's zebras

GRANT'S ZEBRA
Equus quagga boehmi

Grant's zebras have very wide stripes on their hindquarters. Their stripes are dark, and their legs are striped all the way down to their hooves. (A Plains Zebra)

CAPE MOUNTAIN ZEBRA
Equus zebra zebra

Cape Mountain zebras are the smallest zebras, standing only 4 feet at the shoulders (1.2 meters). They have a strip of narrow stripes above the base of the tail, and flaps of skin on their necks called "dewlaps." (A Mountain Zebra)

HARTMANN'S MOUNTAIN ZEBRA
Equus zebra hartmanne

Hartmann's Mountain zebras are taller than Cape Mountain zebras, and their stripes are narrower and closer together. (A Mountain Zebra)

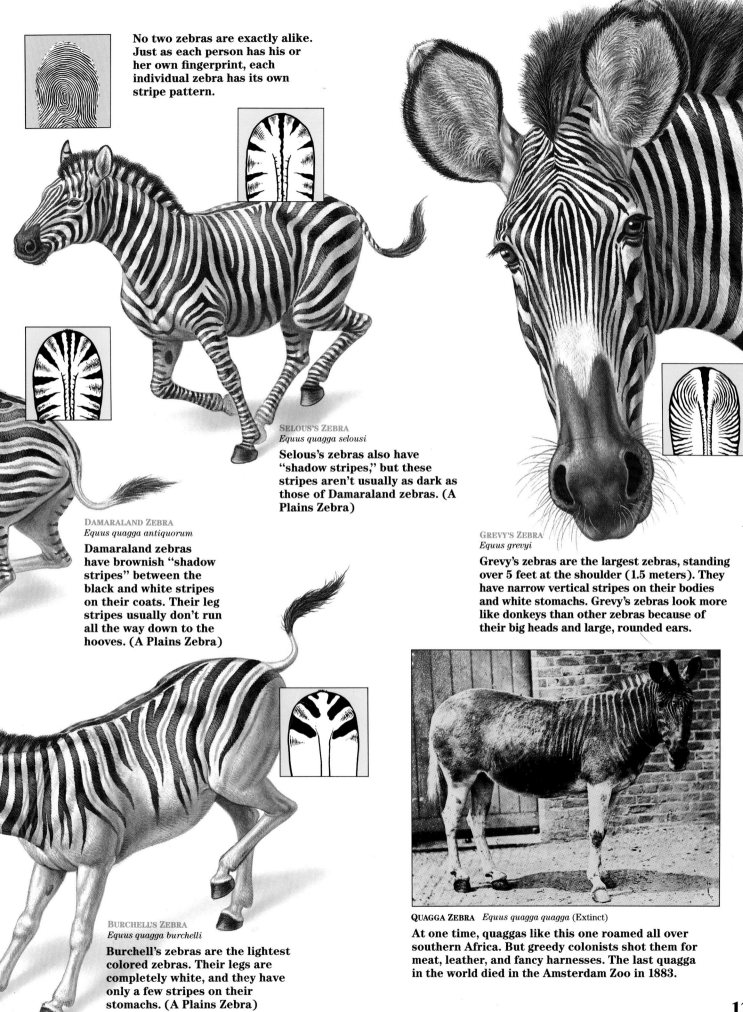

No two zebras are exactly alike. Just as each person has his or her own fingerprint, each individual zebra has its own stripe pattern.

SELOUS'S ZEBRA
Equus quagga selousi

Selous's zebras also have "shadow stripes," but these stripes aren't usually as dark as those of Damaraland zebras. (A Plains Zebra)

DAMARALAND ZEBRA
Equus quagga antiquorum

Damaraland zebras have brownish "shadow stripes" between the black and white stripes on their coats. Their leg stripes usually don't run all the way down to the hooves. (A Plains Zebra)

GREVY'S ZEBRA
Equus grevyi

Grevy's zebras are the largest zebras, standing over 5 feet at the shoulder (1.5 meters). They have narrow vertical stripes on their bodies and white stomachs. Grevy's zebras look more like donkeys than other zebras because of their big heads and large, rounded ears.

BURCHELL'S ZEBRA
Equus quagga burchelli

Burchell's zebras are the lightest colored zebras. Their legs are completely white, and they have only a few stripes on their stomachs. (A Plains Zebra)

QUAGGA ZEBRA *Equus quagga quagga* (Extinct)

At one time, quaggas like this one roamed all over southern Africa. But greedy colonists shot them for meat, leather, and fancy harnesses. The last quagga in the world died in the Amsterdam Zoo in 1883.

13

Zebras are social animals. They live in small groups, or *herds*, of 5 to 15 animals. A herd is usually made up of several females and their young, led by an adult male, or *stallion*.

Living in herds is much safer for zebras than living alone. This is because a group of zebras has many more eyes and ears to watch and listen for predators. Also, if one zebra is in trouble, the others come to its rescue. And if a zebra is missing from the group, all search for it until it is found.

Zebras use the expressions on their faces to let each other know how they feel about things. An angry zebra pulls back its ears and shows its teeth Ⓐ.

A frightened zebra shows its teeth, too—but its ears are pulled *forward* Ⓑ.

These zebras are saying a friendly "hello." Notice how their mouths are open and their ears are pricked up.

Sometimes fights break out between male zebras. Usually the animals try to bite each other on the neck and legs, or they kick each other with their hindlegs. Fighting zebras can hurt each other seriously.

16

Zebras are noisy animals. They "talk" to each other by braying or barking loudly. Individual zebras can recognize each other by their voices. They often call to each other when they are separated.

The front feet of a zebra are more delicate than the back feet. So zebras rarely use their front feet when they fight. The risk of injury is too great.

When a zebra has an itch, it scratches itself by rubbing against a tree, boulder, stump, or even another zebra!

Zebras clean their bodies by rolling in mud or dust! When the mud dries, they shake it off along with loose hair and flakes of dry skin. The film of dust that is left on the skin acts as a shield against heat, wind, and insects.

Wouldn't it be funny if you could clean yourself the way zebras do— by taking a bath in mud?

17

Zebras are grazing animals. Their favorite food is grass. But if necessary, they will eat shrubs, leaves, fruit, roots, and even bark. Since this type of food is low in nutritional value, zebras must eat a lot of it to get the nourishment they need.

For this reason, they spend many hours each day grazing. But they always keep a watchful eye out for trouble. Usually they graze in the morning and late evening. Then at midday, they rest in the shade, standing together in a close group. When all the grass in one area has been eaten, they move on to new pastures.

Birds called oxpeckers help to keep zebras clean by eating the tiny pests that burrow in their skin.

Zebras need to drink water often. When water is scarce, they can sniff out underground pools, dig a hole, and uncover a fresh supply.

Zebras often graze side by side with giraffes and wildebeests. Each animal eats a different type of food, so there is enough for everyone.

Some scientists think that a zebra's stripes help to hide, or *camouflage*, it within the herd. But predators seem to have no trouble picking out one zebra to chase. Do a zebra's stripes really make it harder for predators to see it? We may never know for sure.

When attacked by predators, an alarm call is passed through the herd and all the animals flee. As they run, they stay very close together—with their bodies almost touching. They can run this way for hours, without ever bumping into each other.

Zebras almost never rest in tall grass, because a predator could be hiding there. When they do lie down to rest, one animal —usually a stallion—remains standing to watch for trouble.

19

Baby zebras are called *foals*. Male babies are called *colts*, and females are called *fillies*. A newborn foal weighs 60 to 70 pounds (27 to 32 kilograms), and stands about 3 feet tall (1 meter). Its fur is softer and fuzzier than its mother's. And its stripes are sometimes brown and white, rather than black and white.

A mother zebra watches over her baby carefully, and keeps it close to her at all times. When the baby is very young, she chases away any other zebra that comes near, even the leader of the herd. When the baby grows older, it joins the herd and plays with other young zebras. But even then, it is protected from predators by its mother and other adult zebras.

When danger threatens, the adults push the foals to the inside of the herd to guard them. Then they all take off running, the babies safe within a mass of bodies.

Foals have manes that run down the whole length of their backs—all the way down to their tails. As they get older, the long mane disappears, and an adult mane takes its place. But while they are young, their mother grooms the mane often to show her affection.

Foals spend a lot of time playing. By running fast and pushing and shoving each other in play fights, they develop speed and strength. And they learn how to be leaders and followers, and to run with the herd.

20

When running with the herd, foals always stay close to their mothers for protection. But other zebras will watch over them, too, if necessary.

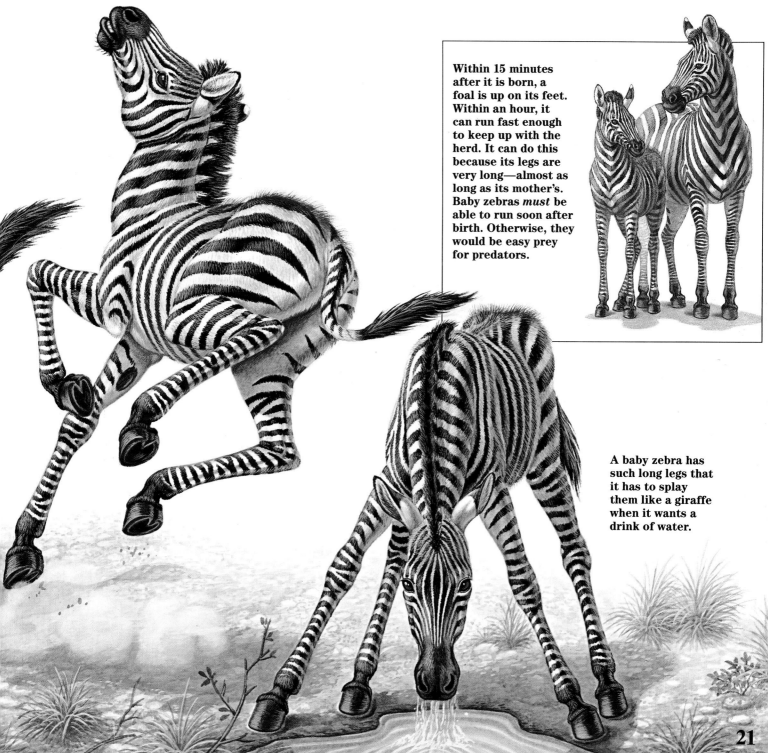

Within 15 minutes after it is born, a foal is up on its feet. Within an hour, it can run fast enough to keep up with the herd. It can do this because its legs are very long—almost as long as its mother's. Baby zebras *must* be able to run soon after birth. Otherwise, they would be easy prey for predators.

A baby zebra has such long legs that it has to splay them like a giraffe when it wants a drink of water.

21

Zebras
FUN!

Everything from A to Zebra is on these two pages of zebra activities. Use what you have learned about zebras to complete these fun exercises!

Q: What's black and white and red all over?

A: An embarrassed zebra, of course.

Zebra Anagrams

Anagrams is a game where scrambled letters are rearranged to form words. A six-letter word related to zebras can be made out of each set of letters on the right. If you can't figure out the six letter zebra word, look for a shorter word. For example, the word *pie* can easily be seen in the first set of letters. To figure out your score, give yourself 2 points for each letter you used. For each word in which you used all six letters, give yourself 20 extra points.

1. S P I E T R
2. C R A F I A
3. S N A I L P
4. V R E G S Y
5. P L A G L O
6. V E S H O O
7. S L O M R A
8. G A G A U Q

Answers

1. stripe   2. Africa   3. plains   4. Grevy's   5. gallop   6. hooves   7. molars   8. quagga

A Zebra Can't Change Its Stripes

Materials: White typing paper and a black felt tip marker or black ink pad.

Make a fingerprint on white paper. First, color your fingertip with a black felt tip marker. Then, press your finger against the white paper. (The print may be clearer the second or third time you press your finger on the paper.)

Collect fingerprints from several different people. Compare the fingerprints. You will find that no two fingerprints are exactly alike. Just imagine—with all the people in the world, no two of them have fingerprints that are exactly the same. This is also true of the stripes of zebras. No two zebras have stripe patterns that are exactly alike.

Art Challenge: Make a row of black fingerprints on white paper. Turn these fingerprints into a herd of zebras by adding heads, legs, and tails with a black felt pen.

22

[There are 71 zebras!]

Read More About Zebras

Wonders of Zebras by Vincent Scuro. New York: Dodd, Mead and Co., 1983.

What's it like to be a zebra in Africa? If you've ever wondered, this lively book is for you. Find out what zebras eat and what their social habits are. Learn more about their anatomy. Great resource for report writing, too.

Zoo Babies: Zelda the Zebra by Georgeanne Irvine. Chicago: Childrens Press, 1982.

Was there any way a baby zebra could lose her stripes? That's what Zelda the zebra wished for herself. You see, she did not want to be like everyone else. Then she learned an important lesson about zebras and their stripes.

Start ▶

Finish ◀

A-MAZING ZEBRAS!

Can you find your way through the maze of stripes created by these five A-Mazing Zebras? There is *only one way* to get from Start to Finish. See if you can find the hidden path.

23

Index

Africa, zebra habitats in, 12
Anger displays by zebras, 16

Baby zebras, 14-15, 20-21
Barking, 17
Behavior of zebras, 8-9, 10-11, 16-17, 20-21
Body structure of zebras, 8-9
Bone structure of zebras, 8-9
Braying, 17
Burchell's Zebra, 13

Camouflage, 19
Cape Mountain Zebra, 12
Colts, 20
Crocodiles, as zebra predators, 11

Damaraland Zebra, 13
Defenses of zebras against predators, 10-11
Drinking behavior, 18

Endangerment of zebras, 6
Equus, 6
Escaping from predators, 10-11
Evolution of zebras, 8-9
Expressions on zebra faces, 16
Extinct zebras, 13
Eyesight, 11

Facial patterns of zebras, 16
Female zebras, 14-15, 21
Fighting
  against predators, 10-11
  among zebras, 16-17
Fillies, 20
Foals, 20
Foot structure, 8-9
Fright behavior, 16

Galloping gait, 8-9
Giraffes, 18-19
Grant's Zebra, 12
Grass
  as a hiding place for predators, 19
  as zebra food, 8, 18-19
Grazing behavior, 18-19
Grevy's Zebra, 6, 13

Habitats of zebras, 6, 8-9, 12
Habits of zebras, 10-11, 16-17, 18-19, 20-21
Hartmann's Mountain Zebra, 12
Hearing ability, 11
Herding behavior, 11, 16-17, 18-19, 20-21
Hindquarters, stripe patterns on, 12-13
Horses, zebras as, 6
Hunting of zebras, 6
Hyenas, as zebra predators, 10

Identifying zebras, 12-13
Itching behavior, 17

Kicking, 10
Kinds of zebras, 12-13

Leg structure, 8-9
  of baby zebras, 21
Leopards, as zebra predators, 10
Lions, as zebra predators, 11, 18-19

Male zebras, 16-17
Mesohippus, 8
Molars, 8
Mountain zebras, 6, 12
Mud baths, 17
Muscles of zebras, 9

Neck structure, 8

Oxpeckers, 18

Plains zebras, 6, 12-13
Plants, as zebra food, 8, 18-19
Playing, 20-21
Predators, defenses of zebras against, 10-11
Protection
  of endangered zebras, 6
  of young zebras, 20-21

Quagga Zebra, 13

Resting, 18
Running styles of zebras, 8-9, 10, 20-21

Scientific names of zebras, 6, 12-13
Selous's Zebra, 13
Senses of zebras, 10-11
Skeleton, 8-9
Smell, 10
Speed of zebras, 8-9
Stallion, 16
Stripes, 6
  patterns of, 12-13

"Talking" among zebras, 17
Teeth, 8
Toe structure, 8
Trotting gait, 8-9

Walking styles of zebras, 8-9
Weights of zebras, 8
  newborn, 20
Wildebeests, 18-19
Wild dogs, as zebra predators, 10